How to Start A Quality Home Daycare Business

7 Steps to Launching your Daycare in 60 days

Copyright © 2020 by DeShonda Jennings

All rights reserved. This book or any portion thereof may not be reproduced or used in any manner whatsoever without the express written permission of the publisher except for the use of brief quotations in a book review.

Printed in the United States of America

First Printing, 2020

ISBN: 978-1-7353320-0-0
Edited & Formatted by Show Your Success
Published by DeShonda Jennings

This book is dedicated to:

My daughter **TyShaunda Leigh-Anah.** She is the reason I started my Home Daycare Business as well as my reason for entering the Early Childhood Field. After being blessed with her nine and a half years after my son (and being told that I could not and would not be able to birth any more children), I didn't trust anyone taking care of my miracle baby while I worked. I felt like a new parent because a lot of what I knew had changed in child development. As I furthered my education, I made a commitment that I would be "that provider" protecting my own and protecting other children as if they were mine as well as working with families. DJ's Shining Stars Daycare was established.

LaCharle', Pumpkin, TyShaunda, Diamond, Tyler, and Damion for sharing your mommy with all the children that attended daycare in our home.

My mother, **Inell Hite,** for being my substitute provider for so many years; for taking all the training that I required beyond what state licensing required; for engaging the children in the best art activities; for your love of reading to all the kids; and for the best home-cooked nutritious meals on Mondays.

And to my dad, the **late Charlie Hite,** for driving one and a half hours one way just to bring my mom down on Sundays so she could work on Monday for me. In some weeks, he drove back the next day to pick her up. He never complained of the long drives.

Acknowledgments

I would like to thank my Aunt Margaret, my cousin Joy, Joyce, and Desiree for making all the fun learning experiences possible; from the local Parks, Around the World restaurants, Museums, Zoo, Strawberry patch, Pumpkin patch, Farms, State Fair, Other Daycare Field Trips, Music and Movement and all the way to Busch Gardens. I am forever grateful. To all the parents and grandparents that trusted me, DJ's Shining Stars Daycare, with your precious babies. Thank you for allowing me to be a part of their lives. Those priceless memories will always be with me.

A special thanks to everyone who pre-ordered a copy of this book:
1. Synqueshia Garnes, North Chesterfield, VA www.thelipstickboutique.com IG:Synqueshia
2. LaCharle' Hazelwood, LPN Chesterfield, VA
3. Makeda King, North Chesterfield, VA
4. Tamekia B. Taylor Four Oaks NC www.sincerelyyoursfr.com
5. Sherry Walker Charlotte NC
6. Dr. Amy Walton Meherrin, VA www.dramywalton.com
7. Inell Hite Victoria VA

Acknowledgments

8. Thomas Jennings Chesterfield VA
9. Geneva Hines Meherrin VA
10. Natisha Hyman North Chesterfield VA Tisha Unique Design
11. Joy Baskerville Meherrin VA
12. Dr. Stevii Aisha Mills, Visibility Coach www.cultivatingyouritfactor.com
13. Diva Moore Living With Divatude, @ LivingWithDivatude
14. Matika Shaw website: Impressivecreditsolutions.com FB:https://www.facebook.com/IPDreams123/
15. Monique Williams
16. Shavonne Johnson North Chesterfield, VA
17. Ethel Burns Dundas, VA
18. Irby & Betty Harrison Bronx, NY
19. KittyKittyBooks Wash your hands Website - https://kittykittybooks.com

Table of Contents

Acknowledgments v

Introduction ix

Chapter 1 Understand the Benefits of Daycare 1

Chapter 2 Set Up Your Business 9

Chapter 3 Get Certified 21

Chapter 4 Develop Policies 29

Chapter 5 Find Families 39

Chapter 6 Hire for Success 45

Chapter 7 Launch 51

Conclusion 59

DJ's Shining Stars Past Parent Testimonials 63

Family Childcare Provider Testimonial 65

Addendum: Guidance from CDC 67

Introduction

Congratulations on purchasing a copy of How to Start A Home Daycare Business.

Research states that Family Day Home Care is the most common form of childcare in this country. This is especially true for younger children. Many parents choose family child care because it's more like a home setting for their child, flexible hours, and they have the same caregiver. Home daycare also has a smaller group size. In my own daycare, I treated each child as if they were my own. It was such a joy to see them grow and develop into their own little personalities. The kids that were enrolled in my program will always have a special place in my heart. There are several different levels of where you may start. After reading to the end, you will be better informed on how you want to proceed and at which level. As we go into each chapter, I will use real-life experiences to explain certain sections. I will share a little of how I got started in the daycare business. Before I go into that, you will need to know:

Disclaimer: This book was written during a Global Pandemic. Follow any social distancing guidelines set by your state. In this book, I am giving you the basic steps that you can follow to start your daycare now. Others in

Introduction

the industry may agree or disagree with my instructions. Child care providers each have their own teaching style. I am also sharing my opinions as well as my real-life experiences and knowledge that I have learned and my ongoing studying of Early Childhood Development and Teacher Education. I am a Certified Childcare Provider. I encourage you to take your daycare to the top.

"The Lack of Affordable Quality child care is a ticking time bomb."

~ Melanne Verveer

CHAPTER 1

Understand the Benefits of Daycare

"Train a child in the way he should go, and when he is old, he will not depart from it".
~ Proverbs 22:6

Understand the Benefits of Daycare

This chapter on the benefits of daycare is very important because it explains how you are a direct impact on a child's future. There are five main points in this chapter that are crucial to the early childhood development of children who will be enrolled in your program. High-quality child care helps children develop skills they will need for success in school and outside school. These skills include but are not limited to social-emotional and communication skills.

Kindergarten Readiness

Being enrolled in daycare prepares children for kindergarten. They are exposed to activities that help to develop cognitive skills, language skills, mathematics skills, motor, and social skills. In my daycare, I had a kindergarten readiness checklist for each preschooler. The kindergarten readiness checklist was broken down into personal development, a section on physical and motor development, literacy and language, mathematics, science, history, and social science. During play and regular instruction in the fall, winter, and spring sessions, I look for skills and knowledge in each of these areas. At the end of each quarter, I held a conference with the parent to discuss the skills and knowledge that was observed. Not only were the findings of the checklist discussed, but I also had samples of their child's work to go along with it.

I provided many opportunities for outside play including jumping with rope, playing games that involve running, catching a ball, bouncing a ball, and overall, just having outside fun. I also had a Writing Center to help prepare the children for kindergarten. I provided materials that help with motor skills such as scissors and paper, crayons, markers, and pencils. One of everyone's favorite activities was playing with Play-Doh. They didn't even realize that I was preparing them for kindergarten by working on their motor skills, cognitive, and social skills. Studies find that by age 5, kids who attended Child Care programs have stronger reading and math skills. To help kids with their reading skills, I had a cozy reading corner in which kids could read books and look at magazines.

Better communicators

Children that attend daycare are better communicators. A quality program can help a child to understand basic vocabulary, speak in complete sentences, recognize letters and numbers, and simple words. Some of the children in my daycare even learned how to print the letters of their name. You will want to have a print-rich environment. It will help the children learn words as they become familiar with annunciating them. I had the names of things printed and posted throughout the room. For example, I had the word 'table' written on a piece of paper attached to the table; I had the word 'door' written on a sentence strip attached to the door. Not only could they see the door, but they could also annunciate and spell the word 'door'. The word 'blocks' was written on the Block Center that way kids could put in perspective an item to a word. I taught basic Spanish words and numbers to the children. The children performed a song in Spanish for their parents. One of my goals was to have a diverse classroom to help with their reading. This also helped them to better communicate and express what they wanted. I also had posters that displayed pictures of kids expressing different feelings. For example, the poster about anger helped kids to better communicate and see what anger looks like. These posters helped kids to visualize and communicate what their feelings were. For other examples of having a print rich environment, go to www.bonusdaycarein60days.com

Healthier Eating Habits

You are in a position to show children what it means to eat for good health and the importance of eating a variety of foods. Research has shown that there are crucial relationships between nutrition and health, and nutrition and learning. By serving nutritious meals and snacks, you help children get the nourishment and energy needed to learn, grow, and be healthy. You play an important role in teaching about healthy food choices. This will encourage some children to maintain a healthy weight as they grow.

Here are a few things you can do:

- Offer a variety of nutritious foods in your plan meals and snack times.
- Eat meals along with them.
- Look for opportunities to discuss the different food groups and the importance of eating foods from all of them.
- Introduce new foods. You may have parents that say 'my child doesn't eat that.' But what I've learned in most cases is that the children had never been introduced to that particular food. In other cases, I used a secret ingredient. Just kidding, it wasn't a secret ingredient. I just prepared it a different way than what they were used to at home.
- I also found a good way of encouraging kids to try something new was to let them help to prepare it. In my experience, kids love making their own snacks and helping with meals. You can introduce a new food by making it an entire learning experience.

This is one of the things that I did when I introduced pumpkin. We took a field trip to the Berry Farm. Each child got to help carve out the classroom pumpkin. We discussed what was inside of the pumpkin, what it was going to feel like, etc. They also got to make homemade pumpkin bread. In that whole pumpkin experience, the children learned that trying something new actually was delicious. They learned social skills by taking turns and working together to make the bread. They learned math because they had to measure out how much flour to put in the bowl. They learned science because they got to see the pumpkin go from a solid to a liquid. They got to use their cognitive skills as we discussed 'what do you think is going to happen next?' They also got to plant pumpkin seeds that they removed from the pumpkin.

Back to healthy eating habits. By having planned meals and snacks at regular times, it helps children to develop good eating patterns. You are a role model for healthy eating. Children like to imitate adults. So, when you eat meals with children, start by eating your vegetables first. They will model what you do.

Regular Schedule and Routines

Children need to know what's next. By having a predictable, regular schedule, it helps to build trust between the childcare provider and children. This also helps children understand that you will take care of their needs regularly. A regular routine brings comfort and consistency to a child's life. Routines also establish expectations. They create a calmer environment.

Be sure to plan activities into your routine that encourages the children's interest. For clarification, your regular schedule should include small group activities,

Understand the Benefits of Daycare

large group activities, free choice time, outdoor time, transition, and routine. Routine is going to be key. Routines should match each child's stage of development. Routines learned in daycare can also be carried over into the home life. Routines contribute to self-esteem as well as independence. More on this topic will be explained in Chapter 7.

Chapter 2

Set up your Business

"To be successful, you have to have your heart in your business, and your business in your heart."
~ Thomas Watson Sr.

Set up your Business

This chapter focuses on setting up your business. When some people think of a home daycare, they think of it as a babysitter. Setting your business up is key. It takes you from a level of being thought of as a babysitter to a child care provider/business owner. Setting up your business is what makes you a professional business owner from the comfort of your home. Setting your business up properly contributes to the success of your business.

Business Structures

There are four main types of businesses. The first type of business is a sole proprietorship. The second type is a partnership. The third type is a limited liability company (LLC). The fourth type is a corporation. The main difference in the structure of your business is the liability on the owner as well as tax advantages and disadvantages.

When I first started my daycare in 2007, my business structure was a sole proprietor. One of the biggest advantages I received by operating as a sole proprietor was that I was able to take deductions on things that I was already paying for. For example, at that time, I could deduct my rent which later moved to my mortgage, utility bills, alarm system, any repairs, and home improvements for the rooms that I used for childcare. I received these deductions because my daycare was considered a home-based business. Although I have a degree in accounting, I would say refer to your tax adviser or CPA as far as which business structure would be best for you.

For the sake of this book, I will focus on setting up your business a sole proprietorship or LLC. It is important to determine which business structure you will like your business to be. With a sole proprietorship, all the liability is on you as the owner. The advantage of operating as an LLC is that the liability will be on the company and not the individual.

As a sole proprietor, the liability fell on me. DeShonda Jennings was solely responsible for the aspects of the business and any liability.

EIN/DUNS Number

There are two types of numbers each business should have. An EIN and a DUNS number. An EIN is nothing more than a federal employee identification number assigned by the IRS. This number is used for businesses for tax filing and reporting purposes. As a sole proprietor, you do not have to necessarily have an EIN. However, you want to obtain an EIN to avoid identity theft and to show that you are a business. Obtaining your EIN is free and easier than most may think. When I obtained my EIN, I simply typed 'IRS' and 'EIN' in the search field. A link came up to apply for an EIN online. Using the online tool was fast and easy. You can also apply for your EIN by fax, email, and telephone. You can also obtain your EIN by simply downloading the IRS form SS4 or by calling the IRS doing their normal operating hours.

Another important number used by businesses is a DUNS number. When I first started my daycare business, I didn't know what a DUNS number was. As I surrounded myself with other business professionals, I later learned the importance of having a DUNS number which is nothing more than a 9 digit number that is recognized as a universal standard to track businesses worldwide. You must request your DUNS number through Dun and Bradstreet which is the largest business credit reporting Bureau. The benefit of establishing a DUNS number for your business is that anyone seeking to better understand your business credit history and creditworthiness would likely look to Dun and Bradstreet to find this information. If you plan to contract with government agencies, then you will be required to have a DUNS number. It increases the credibility of your business and your creditworthiness. Obtaining a DUNS number is also FREE.

Business Bank Account

Every business owner should have a business bank account. When you were just starting out in business, you may have thought it was easier to run your business through your personal checking account. However, to remain professional you want to have a business bank account. When I first started my daycare, this is one of

Set up your Business

the mistakes that I made. I deposited all of my daycare payments into my personal bank account. I also used my personal checking for expenses which made it hard for me to obtain business credit in the beginning because there was no account attached to my business.

I do not want you to make the same mistake that I made. Having a business account also ensures your customers that you are in fact a true business. A business bank account also helps you to keep your records organized. It gives you a better sense of estimating your taxes accurately and keeping track of your deductions. You can also get a merchant account which will allow you to accept credit cards. In all honesty, you just look professional and you can develop bank relationships.

Be sure to do your due diligence in comparing different banks and types of accounts. You want to see which bank is going to have the lowest monthly fee if there is one. You will want to know what the minimum opening deposit will be as well as the minimum daily balance required to waive the monthly fee if there is one. When choosing a bank, determine which offers the best benefits including interest checking, free cashier's checks, free money orders, or business payroll. You should compare two to three banks/bank accounts before making your decision on where to open your account and the type of account.

Set up your Business

Business Plan

Every business needs a business plan. Business plans can be as simple as a two-page plan with potential growth or as detailed as a 20 Page business plan. For in-home daycare, your business plan may be simple or complex. When I first started my home daycare, my business plan was broken into 5 major sections.

- Section 1 is your Business Concept. You will list the general description of the business and your mission statement.
- Section II will include background information such as personal information and ownership as well as skills and experience.
- Section III should include the Description of Services. List your services and program goals in this section.
- Section IV is The Marketing Plan. It lists your target market, competition, and marketing strategies.
- Section V is The Financial Plan. In this section, you would list what is needed for your business. For example, the price/cost of quality indoor and outside equipment. There are many early childhood teacher stores in which you can buy your equipment for your daycare. By purchasing through one of those vendors, you can have a warranty on your equipment as well as you will

Set up your Business

have the assurance that the equipment will be made sturdy and strong.

In your business plan, include the name of your daycare that you established with your business structure. In section II, provide a summary of the history of your company including the year it was established as well as the business structure and the county in which it was established.

In section III, list your company goals and objectives. You also want to give a little information about the ownership background. For example, you want to include information about who you are. If you are a mother with kids, how many kids do you have, what makes you credible, and your education? You also want to advise the target for your product which for daycare, your service is going to be quality and affordable child care.

In section IV, identify who the target market is, pricing, advertising, and competitor analysis. What other daycares are around you? Are they in-home daycares? Centers? After school programs? Include the range of businesses that you have evaluated such as within 5 miles of your in-home daycare. Be sure to also include how many staff are need for each age range of children. For example, from birth to 16 months the ratio was one thing while up to school age is another.

Be sure to include an Executive Summary in your Business Plan.

Set up your Business

Have your files setup

You should have your children's files already set up and ready for enrollment. I personally like to use file folders. In the front of the file folder, I have a checklist that lists what should be included in the folder. This is called your enrollment packet. Your enrollment form should have a space to put the child's complete name, sex, date of birth, and home address. The child enrollment form should also list the parents' names, phone number, work address, and work phone number. You will want to have a section to list two emergency contacts preferably one local and another outside of the area. Be sure to have a section that lists the name, address, telephone number. Your file should also have a blank copy of a school interest form which has a section for a physical as well as immunization record. In your file, you should have a blank authorization to administer medication as well as a permission slip record. Remember, you don't have to create the forms. Many blank child enrollment forms may be downloaded from your local department of social services website. Most states also have childcare networks that will provide sample forms as well. In your file, you will need a parent contract. Parent contracts will be discussed in Chapter 4. For sample enrollment forms go to www.Bonusdaycarein60days.com.

What is your goal number of families, prices, age range?

You need to know the goal number of families and your price per age range. In other words, how many families do you want to enroll as well as how much will you charge per child?

When I first left my job in corporate America, I figured out the amount of money that I would need to pay my bills. This gave me an idea of what I needed to charge per child. I also checked with other child care providers within a 5 to 10-mile radius from where I lived. Because I was new to the childcare field, I actually undercut myself. Do not make the mistake that I made by undervaluing yourself. Your prices should be based on what you bring to the table or what experience do you have in the field and the quality of the program that you will be offering parents.

Another thing to consider is a rate for full-time as well as part-time children. If you're going to start out working by yourself without an assistant, you can only have a certain number of children enrolled. Check with your local Zoning for state-specific information. Create a rate table to include a rate for full-time children, part-time children, and daily rates which were used for drop-ins. For examples of rate schedules, go to www.Bonusdaycarein60days.com.

Business Set-Up Checklist:

Note: Not all items may apply. This list doesn't mean this is the order in which you should do things. This checklist is to be used as a guide on what you have completed or need to complete to set up your business.

- ❑ Business Name
- ❑ Business Address
- ❑ Business Number
- ❑ Business Entity
- ❑ EIN Number
- ❑ DUNS Number
- ❑ Business License/Permits
- ❑ Bank Account
- ❑ Business Plan
- ❑ Business Insurance
- ❑ Tax Advisor
- ❑ Other

Business Resources:

Matika Shaw website: Impressivecreditsolutions.com
FB:https://www.facebook.com/IPDreams123/

Sherry Walker
Insure Tax NC
www.insuretaxnc.biz

Jackson Insurance Services
Cal Jackson
cal@jacksoninsuranceserv.com

CHAPTER 3

Get Certified

"The beautiful thing about learning is that no one can take it away from you."

~ BB King

This chapter is about different ways to be certified. Families need to know that you are taking the proper steps to keep their children safe by providing a safe environment. Learning doesn't stop here. Professional development is ongoing for regulations and research changes frequently. Set high standards now so when you become regulated, you will have a competitive advantage over other providers.

Check with your local zoning

Based on the state in which you live, you may need to check with your local zoning office. In the state of Virginia where I reside, a family day home caring for more than four children under the age of 2 shall be licensed or voluntarily registered. A family day home where the children in care are all related to the provider by blood or marriage should not be required to be licensed. Each state has specific guidelines. As far as business licensing is concerned, it depends on the state that you live in. Some business license applications will require that you have already received your family child care license from the state. If that is the case, you want to apply for the business license after the state family child care license. In some states, the family child care license application might require that you already have a business license before applying.

If your goal is to become state-licensed or voluntarily registered for your state, schedule a one-on-one session with me by going to www.startadaycarein60days.com

Get the right insurance

Liability protection for your home daycare is a must. As a small business owner, it is your responsibility to make sure you have the right insurance in place to protect your business from the unexpected.

Daycare Insurance can help cover any legal costs in the event of a lawsuit. Remember accidents can happen even if you're not at fault therefore, you need to protect yourself and your business from these expenses. You may ask the question, "what if I have homeowners insurance? Would I still need liability protection for my daycare?" The answer is 'yes'. In fact, most homeowner's insurance policies do not cover a daycare business.

The coverage you choose also depends on the set up of your home daycare. If you already have several children in your care, you should consider a commercial policy. A standard home daycare endorsement only applies if you are the sole proprietor. If your business expands and you hire employees, you should get a commercial insurance policy.

Get your certifications (CPR/First aid/MAT)

The main certifications that you should have before opening your daycare are to be CPR (cardiopulmonary resuscitation) and First Aid certified. If you would like to administer certain medications, you should also be MAT certified. CPR is a life-saving technique. The MAT program trains and certifies providers to safely administer medications to children in their care provided you have written permission from the parent. Some of the topics covered in the MAT course are an overview of medication effects. You will learn ways to give both over-the-counter and prescription medications. You will learn how to handle, store, and safely dispose of medication. Other skills learned would be the permission and instruction requirements, preparation and administration techniques, and Asthma emergency care and special situations. For assistance with state-specific guidelines on the MAT program, schedule a Discovery session at www.startadaycarein60days.com

Register with your local Child and Adult Food Care Program

One of the additional services that I provided in my daycare was FREE breakfast, lunch, and snacks to all children enrolled. This was a benefit to many families because parents did not have to worry about packing a child's lunch, feeding their child breakfast before dropping off in the morning, or packing a snack for the afternoon. Most importantly, they knew their child was receiving healthy nutritious meals. I did not have to increase my rates. I received reimbursement for providing meals because I was registered with my local child and adult food program (CACFP). The CACFP is a Federal program that provides reimbursement for nutritious meals and snacks to eligible children. By participating in the USDA which is part of the CACFP program, parents will be aware that their child is receiving the proper number of servings for milk, fruits and vegetables, meats, and grains. There are certain criteria for you to be approved to participate. This is determined by the level at which you choose to operate your business.

Home inspection

A home inspection is a safety walk to your business. There are two major types of Home Inspections. The one I will be telling you about is the one you can do yourself. You can have a health and safety checklist. I suggest having it visible to parents so they can see the steps that you are taking to keep their children safe. In my daycare, I did my safety checks daily. I did an indoor checklist every morning before opening. The outside safety check was completed at the end of each day and before taking the children outside.

Get Certified

Areas to check and inspect include any space the children will be present including but not limited to indoor hallways, toys, equipment, bathroom, and outside area. If you find something that could be a hazard, correct it immediately or remove it. Remember parents are trusting you to keep their children safe. For a sample safety checklist, go to www.Bonusdaycarein60days.com.

The second type of home inspection is the one conducted by the division of Licensing programs. This inspection goes into greater detail checking the complete physical environment and equipment in your home. Each state has very specific standards. For assistance in getting an in-home inspection conducted by your State, schedule a one-on-one session with me at www.startadaycarein60days.com

You must get trained

Other types of training will be beneficial to your business. Although I had been a mom for 13 years, I did not know everything that I needed to be sure I was giving the children everything to help with their development. One of the first things that I did was I enrolled in classes at my local Community College. I learned so much that I continued my studies and received a degree in early childhood development. Remember professional development should be ongoing. Your training should include subjects such as growth and development, family, communication, and nutrition. Training on business

Get Certified

management and budgeting will also help you. If you decide to become approved to participate with your local USDA (CACFP) they also offer free training on nutrition. Your local Department of Social Services website has lots of training and professional development available. When you move towards state licensing, the number of required hours will be determined by your State's Division of Licensing programs. For assistance on obtaining a license for your state, schedule a strategy session at startadaycarein60days.com

Chapter 4

Develop Policies

"Our goals can only be reached through the vehicle of a plan. There's no other routes to success."

~ Pablo Picasso

Develop Policies

According to the Merriam-Webster Dictionary, the definition of policy is a definite course or method of action selected from among alternatives and in light of given conditions to guide and determine present and future decisions.

Each of the policies discussed below is considered the roadmap to your daycare business and are important to your daycare business. Parents need to have a clear understanding of the services you are providing and the reason why there's a policy for that particular service. By having policies in effect, it creates transparency between the provider and the parents. In other words, the provider and parents would work together for the benefit of the child. Each of the policies should be thoroughly covered with parents. The parent handbook is your primary policy made up of smaller/secondary policies.

Parent Handbook

As you continue to develop your policies, you must have a parent handbook. What should be included? Your parent handbook should include your daycare name, phone number, and hours of operation. A detailed message explaining your expectations of parents. I know you are probably wondering 'why do I need to explain my expectations?' Remember you may have parents that are enrolling their child in daycare for the first time, they may not know what to expect in a daycare or what not to expect.

Develop Policies

You will also want to list your philosophy or the mission of your daycare to be sure that it is a good fit for what parents are looking for in a daycare. For example, if part of your mission is to start the kids' morning with prayer, someone who may not believe in prayer would not want to have that child engaged in this way. It is also a good idea to have registration information to include fees, annual fees, drop-in rates, attendance blocks, and your absence policy. In my handbook, I had a section on the trial period which was nothing more than the first two weeks of childcare would be on a trial basis. After the two weeks, the parent and provider would decide together if it was the best situation for everyone. If the parent or the child was unhappy or cannot adjust to the program, either party could end the contract with a one-day notice. After the two weeks, the contract will be considered binding and in effect.

You should also list all holiday closings for the year as well as any information about vacation. I found this to be helpful to parents. They were able to make arrangements in advance on the days that the daycare will be closed. In all honesty, no one wants to bring their child to daycare on a Monday and you say, 'oh yeah I'm closed tomorrow.' That's just unprofessional as well as inconsiderate to families.

Your handbook should also state your withdrawal policy which explains to parents the steps to take if they wish to withdraw their child. The handbook also includes a behavior and discipline policy. Your behavior and discipline policy should clearly explain what is expected of children and what actions/steps are taken to redirect the child if needed. Your handbook needs to have specific instructions on the release of children. I included a copy of the Daily Schedule in my handbook. My handbook was designed so that parents could have all information in one document. At the end of your handbook, you should include a Handbook Signature Page for parents to sign and date acknowledging that they have read and received a copy of the handbook. Parents' signatures also acknowledge that they understand all the policies and have had the opportunity to ask any questions for clarification. On the bottom of the page, there is a line for the provider to sign and date. The provider signature acknowledges that they have allowed the parent to ask any questions for clarification.

Outdoor Play Policy

Can you think back to your own outdoor play experiences? I remember making mud pies, building forts, and pretending to be on the beach with a towel on the grass. . Children need to create outdoor memories too. However, there may be times in which the weather does not permit that. This is why you want to have an outdoor play policy in effect. Your policy should be very specific. It should list the temperature range with the amount of time that the children will play outside. You should also list if parents need to send in jackets, hats, and mittens on cold days. You may also want to put a clause in the space to not send your child in a new outfit and shoes if you intend for them not to get dirty. Encourage parents to dress their children for success and exploration.

Illness Policy

This policy specifies when a child may be excluded from daycare. Some of the reasons to exclude are but are not limited to a high temperature of 100 or greater, recurrent vomiting or diarrhea, and any symptoms of communicable diseases. Go to www.Bonusdaycarein60days.com for the Department of Health's list of communicable diseases. Specific instructions explaining what parents are to do if their child becomes ill will be listed under this policy.

Emergency Preparedness

One of my favorite quotes is by Will Smith. "Stay ready so you don't have to get ready." Every child care program must have an emergency preparedness plan in place. Many different types of emergencies could occur at any given time. The first thing that should be included in your plan is a person that will be able to provide emergency backup care. This person should be an approved and reliable adult that can arrive at your home within

Develop Policies

10 minutes. In this section of your plan, you will want to list the adult's full name, complete address, and phone numbers. Most importantly make sure that that adult is aware that they are your backup caregiver. You wouldn't want to just put down a reliable person's name and they don't know anything about the fact that they're on your emergency plan. Makes Sense.

Your plan will consist of three basic responses in the event of an emergency: Evacuate, Shelter-in-place, and Relocate. Each basic response will have clear, detailed instructions on the provider's role, the back up caregiver's role, the safety and supervision of children during the emergency, and ways that parents will be notified. One of the things I did in my daycare was each month we practiced an evacuation drill. We also practiced shelter in place three times a year. In addition to that, I had an emergency bag that included a complete copy of each child's file along with emergency supplies. I used a backpack which made it easy and my hands could stay free. In my outside shed, I also had what I called an emergency evacuation tote in which I had snacks, water, blankets, wipes, diapers, coloring books, crayons, books, etc. Just in case there was an emergency, the tote was easily accessible. Supplies were checked monthly including dates on snacks. For a sample Emergency preparedness plan and suggested Emergency Supplies list, go to www.Bonusdaycarein60days.com

Safety/Sanitation policy

I went a step beyond my safety/inspection checklist and developed a safety and sanitation policy. The purpose of the safety and sanitation policy was to ensure that germs were not spread from one individual to another. Believe it or not, as I write this chapter, I'm looking back in my notes to when I developed this policy; November 2007. It is now May 2020 and one of the things that they're talking about in the world pandemic to stop the spread of the virus is to wash hands often which coincides with the same steps in my policy. Keep in mind this policy was developed in 2007. This policy lists the specific steps that you will take. It also has specific steps for children. Personal toys from home will not be allowed since you have no way to verify that the toys were cleaned and sanitized.

Infant Sleep Policy

Providing infants with a safe place to grow and learn is very important. For this reason, you should create a policy on safe sleep practices for infants up to one-year-old. Follow the recommendations of the American Academy of Pediatrics and the consumer product safety commission to provide a safe sleep environment and reduce the risk of sudden infant death syndrome (SIDS). This sleep policy will list specific guidelines to include the sleep position, the sleep environment, and supervision while they are sleeping. The policy will also list the

Develop Policies

training guidelines for sleep policies and practices. This policy includes the communication plan for provider staff when applicable and parents. Parents are asked to follow the same policy when the infant is at home. The policy will be signed off by you the owner, a health professional consultant if appropriate, staff members are applicable. It is best practice to review this policy annually. For a FREE complete detailed sample Infant Sleep Policy, www.Bonusdaycarein60days.com.

CHAPTER 5

Know Where to Find Families

"Family is not an important thing. It's everything."
~ Michael J. Fox

Know Where to Find Families

You have now completed the first steps to starting your business. It's time to find families. I know you're thinking, "where do I find families?" In this chapter, you will learn about the different ways that you can find families to offer your services to. I want to be very transparent with you. Some may not like what I'm about to say. Be mindful of people who may not respect you as a business owner. They may see you as Ms. so and so (babysitter), not as a professional child care provider.

Existing Providers

There are plenty of children in your community for everyone so don't be afraid to reach out to an existing provider. "Your gift will make room for you" Proverbs 18:16 The truth of the matter is, the max number that one can have an in-home daycare is 12. Based on the state you live in and your zoning, your number may be less. As you begin to reach out to providers, get to know them. They once started where you are starting at. During my years as a child care provider, I built meaningful relationships with many providers. Quite a few have sent referrals to me. As I built my business and maxed out my capacity, I began to send referrals to other providers. Now that I think about it, I had a couple of incidents in which I didn't have space for children and the same provider that I referred the family to, that provider had initially referred that family to me.

Existing providers will also be a good resource to take a look at your daycare setup. A second set of eyes is always best. They also can share with you how they found families when they first got started. Ask them if there is a local childcare association. If so, join it. This is another great opportunity to get referrals. Be sure to read an awesome testimonial from another Family Childcare Provider in the bonus section.

Referral Agencies

Referral agencies are another good resource to get your name out there. Each state has agencies in which providers can register their daycare. There are national nonprofit organizations that have memberships in which parents and providers register for access. You register your daycare information. Parents use those sites to help find quality child care.

Your local department of Social Services is another agency to register with. To have your daycare listed, you will need to be a licensed Family Day Home or a Voluntary Registered Family Day Home. No worries, I've been on both sides and will help you. The way the Department of Social Services site works is that families search by facility name/provider name, county, or zip code. They also will be able to search under the category. For example, if you're registered as a Home Base, Family Day Home, or Voluntary Registered, when you're approved to participate in the food program, they too will have a database in which your information will be available for parents.

Pound the pavement!

There is nothing wrong with walking the streets to find your families. I remember just like it was yesterday. When I relocated to a different subdivision, I lost a few families because my location wasn't convenient for them and in a different school zone. However, it was one of the greatest moves that I made thus far. Back to the streets I went. I made 100 Flyers and walked my entire subdivision putting out flyers. Even though I knew I could only take a specific number of families, I put a flyer on every mailbox in my subdivision until I ran out of flyers. I kid you not, I went from Max Capacity of 12 to a waiting list. I was able to share the overflow with neighboring providers.

Join Parent Groups and Network

The elementary schools within your area are a great place to start. Most schools have parent groups such as the PTA, Parent-Teacher Association, and PTO, Parent-Teacher Organization. Form a relationship with the parents. I'm sure they know of families looking for childcare. The year that my second daughter started kindergarten, I was elected as vice president of the PTA. I got to meet another awesome lady who at that time was the president of the PTA. She too was an in-home provider.

Know Where to Find Families

She had just recently started her home daycare in VA. By connecting with her through the parent group, she and I both always had our ears and eyes open for families looking for daycare. In fact, we became close friends and a huge advocate for children. I was also a Girl Scout leader for over 8 years. I met a lot of parents looking for family child care close to their kids' school.

As Reid Hoffman says "Help the people in your network and let them help you".

As you reflect on that quote, think about all the people that you network with. Don't be afraid to let people know you're starting a daycare and ask if they know anyone who is looking for childcare particularly quality childcare. That is what's going to set you aside from others. You would be surprised at the number of people actually looking for someone that they trust to care for their child. As the old saying goes, 'a closed mouth doesn't get fed.' You cannot assume that people know you're in the business of childcare. Let people know. Social media has many groups set up by parents. Join some of these groups and tell them a little about yourself and what you do. By no means am I saying to go on social media and spam groups. When you join these different groups, introduce yourself, build a relationship, and tell them about how you got into the childcare business. It is okay to let them know that you're new to the field. You always want to be transparent because it builds credibility.

CHAPTER 6

Hire for Success

"Somebody once said that in looking for people to hire, you look for three qualities: integrity, intelligence, and energy. And if you don't have the first, the other two will kill you."

~ Warren Buffett

This chapter is important because you may need to hire an assistant to help provide care. The need for an assistant will be based on your ratio. When I first started my daycare, it was just me and that quickly changed a few months after I opened up. I had to start the hiring process. You will also need a substitute provider in case you have appointments and of course, when you take your vacation. This chapter will give you the details and guidelines on who is qualified to work for you. Remember your first responsibility is the safety and well-being of each child in your care. Anyone, including family members, that you wish to hire or that will have unsupervised access to the children should have the following background checks done.

Background Checks

Federal Law requires ALL states to implement state and federal criminal background checks that include fingerprints for childcare providers. The comprehensive background check must include a fingerprint check of the Federal Bureau of Investigations (FBI) database. This is done to ensure that providers do not have a history of convictions that could put children's health and safety at risk.

The following is a list of the specific checks that are required.

- FBI fingerprint check

- A search of the National Crime Information Center's National Sex Offender Registry
- State child abuse and neglect registry and database
- State sex offender registry or repository
- State criminal history check6

*Note most of these same background checks should be done on any adult that lives in your home. For guidance on state-specific guidelines, schedule a strategy session with me at www.startadaycarein60days.com

Qualifications

The individual that you hire as your substitute should be at least 18 years of age. They should have a high school diploma or higher. Most states require a minimum of three months of experience. In my opinion, you should look for someone with at least a minimum of one year of experience. Remember you are starting a quality daycare. Your standards should be higher than the state's minimum. Be sure their experience matches your business. For example, someone that has experience working with teens does not mean they know how to care for infants.

Do your reference checks to verify their experience. You are responsible for the safety and well-being of the children in your care. The individual needs to be CPR and First Aid Certified. Since they will be running your business in your absence, they need to be able to respond to an emergency. Some states allow an assistant to be 16 as long as they are working directly under you. Keep in mind the 16-year-old may or may not have the experience. This is a great opportunity to mentor that person as you continue to grow in this field.

Your substitute and assistant should have a TB screening. Advise them upfront that ongoing training will be required. There are state-specific required training (professional development) hours. In my program, I went beyond what the state required insisting that my staff obtain a set number of hours of training per quarter. Whatever is your state's minimum, I challenge you to increase it by an additional 6 hours. The training should include a mixture of topics relating to child development, activities, safety, and special needs.

> **"Do not hire a man who does your work for money, but him who does it for the Love of it."**
> ~ **Henry David Thoreau**

Chapter 7

Launch

"Education begins the moment we see children as innately wise and capable beings. Only then can we play along in their world."

~ Vince Gowman

This chapter is about setting it in motion using everything you have learned from training and certifications as well as your policies. Let's get your environment set. It's time to bring the kids in. This chapter is very important because you will be putting in action everything that you have learned thus far. Let's dive right In.

Age Appropriate Curriculum

Age-appropriate curriculum is important because it's about creating learning that is at a child's level of understanding and readiness to learn. The curriculum describes what you want the children in your care to learn as well as the order in which you will teach it. It is also the child's outcome. You can teach the curriculum in several different ways. It is best practice to teach in ways that are "evidence-based". In other words, the approach is effective in helping children learn. Some approaches include intentional teaching, during play, child-initiated activities, teacher-directed activities, and parent engagement.

The curriculum can be delivered anywhere the children are engaged in learning and developing.

A few things to consider when choosing or developing your own curriculum include:

1. Does the curriculum define the roles of the teacher and child?

2. Is the curriculum appropriate for all teachers or would you need additional training?
3. Does the curriculum include parent involvement? What domains of learning are addressed? Domains of learning are cognitive (thinking), affective (social, emotional, feeling), and psychomotor (physical, kinesthetic)
4. Does the curriculum provide an assessment? Remember, whatever curriculum you decide on, it should be based on current research. For assistance on implementing or developing your curriculum, go to www.startadaycarein60days.com for a strategy session.

Centers Arrangement

For clarification purposes, when I use the term 'classroom' I'm talking about the space in which you will be doing your daycare. The words 'centers' and 'stations' are the same, and through them, children will do the most learning. The layout of your centers does affect the way the children use materials as well as the way you would be able to facilitate teaching. Remember kids learn through play. Your center arrangement should be well-planned focusing on the children's safety and their emotional security. Be sure you have enough space so kids can freely move without bumping into each other. Include centers that will encourage cognition and problem solving, social and emotional skills, speech and language development, fine and gross motor skills. Last but most important in my opinion, is diversity. Some of the centers that you should have are Math and manipulatives, Reading, Dramatic play, Blocks, Science, Art and Writing, Music, and Movement. I also had mobile centers. If you don't have enough space to have stations/centers available for most of the day, you could rotate. For example, mini sand and water tables for inside play. When you set up your centers, do not put the block center beside the reading center/cozy corner. The reading center should be as far away from the busiest/loudest area. Kids need an area for relaxation. That's another training in itself. For specific guidance on the center arrangement, schedule a one-on-one session with me. For a suggested list of materials to include in your centers, go to www.Bonusdaycarein60days.com

Plan/Develop Daily Schedule

A daily schedule is nothing more than the order or time of activities that the children will be participating in. This schedule will repeat daily. You need to plan the following into your schedule: greeting the children, breakfast, indoor activities, lunch diapering, toileting, nap, snacks, free play, outdoor activities, and departure. There are a few key points you need to remember when you plan your schedule. Although this is your daily plan, it may be adjusted as needed since you should meet the needs of each child. For example, it may need to be adjusted for a child with special needs or if a preschooler is tired before naptime and needs to nap earlier.

Have your daily activities planned and ready to go. This will make transitions go smoothly for the most part. For example, if the children have washed their hands for lunch, have lunch ready for them. By having them sitting at the table waiting for you to prepare lunch, it could cause a little behavior or playing with materials (then they would have to wash their hands again). Remember children learn through play. If you notice they have taken the chairs and made a school bus, you can make this a teachable moment by playing along with them. For example, you could ask them 'may I please get a ride on the school bus? Or will you take me to school please?' Have some books in your hand so it looks like you are going to school. Then say "Oh I have to buckle my seatbelt. Remember whenever we are riding in a car or truck or bus our seat belts must be buckled. We have to sit on our bottom.' This teaches respect and manners, encourages language and cognitive skills. Ask them 'where is the bus going today?' You would be so surprised by their imagination.

By pretending to ride to school on their bus, it turned into a whole lesson on safety. As you continue to play along, you can ask prompting questions 'how far is the school? What time will you pick me back up?' The things that you could teach the kids are endless all while engaging in play alongside them. For samples of daily schedules, go to www.Bonusdaycarein60days.com

Open House

In this chapter, I explain a "Pre-opening" Open House. This is the time that you have set aside for potential families to view your daycare and ask you questions to see if you are a good fit for them. First impressions are important. Make it count. Even though some of the families may be complete strangers, you can still create a connection. One of the advantages that helped me is that I too am a mom. I thought of all the questions that I would ask. I then incorporated that into my interview (you really are being interviewed during open house) and talked as I walked them around my daycare. They also will be observing your environment looking to see if anything is unsafe, dirty. I know you don't have to worry about that since you have already done your safety home inspection.

You should plan in advance. Make flyers. Share your flyers at the local libraries, with the parents in your parent groups, social media, and any networking events that you attend. Your flyers should have the date, time, location, name, and contact information. When I did my flyers, I listed a few of my credentials. You could offer a special on your registration fee. Have some of your pre-made files/enrollment packets ready. Have refreshments available.

I suggest keeping it simple: a variety of fresh fruit and small bottles of water. Have everything ready as if it is opening day. Most of the little people will be ready to go at it. Some may be shy. As you greet the children, sit down and introduce yourself so that you are on their level as opposed to this tall, unfamiliar person looking over them. Make sense? A family intake form should be available. Remember to encourage each family to fill it out. You should have blocks to capture the following information: parent name, phone number, email, child's name, age, number of kids to enroll, type of service they are looking for, and potential start date. This form will be used as a follow up as well as an indication if you need to hire an assistant. Remember as a provider you have to stay within ratios.

Conclusion

Congratulations! You made it to the end. Be sure to take advantage of all the FREE bonuses by going to www.Bonusdaycarein60days.com. Don't stop here. Let me help you take your home daycare to another level. Don't waste time searching the internet on what to do next. When you are ready for transformation and to take your daycare to another level, contact me if you want results. I once started with the idea of opening a home daycare. I'm sure you can continue to Google and get information but why not work with me to hold you accountable and offer you support as you achieve your goals? Whether you will be operating your at-home daycare as a Home Base, Family Day Home, or Voluntary Registered, go to www.startadaycarein60days.com to schedule your strategy session. Congratulations again!

Resource:

KittyKittyBooks
Wash your hands
Website - https://kittykittybooks.com

Parent Testimonials from DJ'S Shining Stars Daycare

When I moved to Chesterfield in 2009, I didn't have family or friends who lived in the area. But I had to find childcare for my two daughters for me to work a full-time job. I was introduced to DeShonda Jennings from "DJ's Shining Stars". Everything was extremely professional. She welcomed my children and me with open arms. Her establishment was amazing and the setting was awesome. I felt a sense of ease while deciding if I would allow DeShonda to care for my daughters. It was the best decision that I made. In 2011, I had another daughter, and Deshonda was still available to care for my newborn so I could continue to work my full-time job. Not only did she take care of my daughters, but she also helped them with potty training, learning their ABC's, learning how to read and write at such a young age, and she taught them respect. As a single mother, DeShonda has played a major role in my life as well as my kids. "DJ's SHINING STARS" allowed my daughters to grow up in a school setting that prepared them for a real future!! Today they are 16,

Parent Testimonials from DJ'S Shining Stars Daycare

13 and 8 years old and they still LOVE them some MISS DEEDEE!!!

Synqueshia Garnes, North Chesterfield VA

I was so glad when you came to me and told me you were opening a Day Care and I told you my three would be in your care. You helped me out so much and I truly do appreciate it. My children learned so much from being in your daycare. They still talk about the days when they were at DJ's Shining Stars.

Makeda King, North Chesterfield VA

My daughter Zee's experience at DJ's Shining Stars was great. It taught her manners and how to get along with others. The age-appropriate activities Mrs. Dee did with the children helped her so much when she entered PreK the teachers were amazed at how much she knew. She is now 10 and has made honor roll on every report card and has been recommended for advanced math as she will enter the sixth grade this year. Thanks, Mrs. Dee, for being a great 1st teacher to my daughter.

Joy Baskerville, Meherrin VA

Family Childcare Providers

Name of Family Day Home and number of years in business?
I've never had a formal business name, I just operate under my name, but of course most have dubbed it "Ms. Kim's Daycare." I opened in September 2007, so almost 13 years.

What is one of the biggest challenges you have faced in your business as of May 2020?
I think the biggest challenge overall was getting started. Trying to navigate how/where to find clients, deciding what would be a fair and competitive pricing, writing up that first contract and ensuring all your bases are covered.

What is one of your greatest accomplishments or achievements as of May 2020?
I'm proud of the fact that I've built a solid, reputable business. I no longer have to go out seeking clients and am fortunate enough to operate strictly on referrals and "repeat business," to the extent that I have a continual waiting list of interested clients.

If you had to choose one piece of advice for a new provider or an aspiring provider, what would it be?
Create a contract and ENFORCE IT. Please don't start your business without a contract for the protection of all parties involved. Make sure you specify tuition, late fees/penalties (for tuition and for early/late drop-off/pick-up), sick and vacation policies, and specific care hours. Know your worth - your time and the service you provide are valuable.

Owner Name: Owner Name: Kimberly Johnson
Website: N/A
Email: kcj1007@gmail.com
Business Number: 804-690-2324

Addendum

Disclaimer: This book was written during a Global Pandemic in May 2020. The following guidance is directly from the CDC for childcare programs.

Social Distancing Strategies

Work with your local health officials to determine a set of strategies appropriate for your community's situation. Continue using preparedness strategies and consider the following social distancing strategies:

- If possible, child care classes should include the same group each day, and the same child care providers should remain with the same group each day. If your child care program remains open, consider creating a separate classroom or group for the children of healthcare workers and other first responders. If your program is unable to create a separate classroom, consider serving only the children of healthcare workers and first responders.
- Cancel or postpone special events such as festivals, holiday events, and special performances.
- Consider whether to alter or halt daily group activities that may promote transmission.

Addendum

- ◇ Keep each group of children in a separate room.
- ◇ Limit the mixing of children, such as staggering playground times and keeping groups separate for special activities such as art, music, and exercising.
- ◇ If possible, at nap time, ensure that children's naptime mats (or cribs) are spaced out as much as possible, ideally 6 feet apart. Consider placing children head to toe in order to further reduce the potential for viral spread.
- Consider staggering arrival and drop off times and/or have child care providers come outside the facility to pick up the children as they arrive. Your plan for curb side drop off and pick up should limit direct contact between parents and staff members and adhere to social distancing recommendations.
- If possible, arrange for administrative staff to telework from their homes.

Parent Drop-Off and Pick-Up

- Hand hygiene stations should be set up at the entrance of the facility, so that children can clean their hands before they enter. If a sink with soap and water is not available, provide hand sanitizer with at least 60% alcohol next to parent sign-in

sheets. Keep hand sanitizer out of children's reach and supervise use. If possible, place sign-in stations outside, and provide sanitary wipes for cleaning pens between each use.
- Consider staggering arrival and drop off times and plan to limit direct contact with parents as much as possible.
  ◇ Have child care providers greet children outside as they arrive.
  ◇ Designate a parent to be the drop off/pick up volunteer to walk all children to their classroom, and at the end of the day, walk all children back to their cars.
  ◇ Infants could be transported in their car seats. Store car seat out of children's reach.
- Ideally, the same parent or designated person should drop off and pick up the child every day. If possible, older people such as grandparents or those with serious underlying medical conditions should not pick up children, because they are more at risk for severe illness from COVID-19.

Screen Children Upon Arrival (if possible)

Persons who have a fever of 100.40 (38.00C) or above or other signs of illness should not be admitted to the facility. Encourage parents to be on the alert for signs of illness in their children and to keep them home when they are sick. Screen children upon arrival, if possible.

There are several methods that facilities can use to protect their workers while conducting temperature screenings. The most protective methods incorporate social distancing (maintaining a distance of 6 feet from others) or physical barriers to eliminate or minimize exposures due to close contact to a child who has symptoms during screening.

Example of Screening Methods

Reliance on Social Distancing (example)

- Ask parents/guardians to take their child's temperature either before coming to the facility or upon arrival at the facility. Upon their arrival, stand at least 6 feet away from the parent/guardian and child.
- Ask the parent/guardian to confirm that the child does not have fever, shortness of breath or cough.
- Make a visual inspection of the child for signs of illness which could include flushed cheeks, rapid breathing or difficulty breathing (without recent physical activity), fatigue, or extreme fussiness.

You do not need to wear personal protective equipment (PPE) if you can maintain a distance of 6 feet.

www.ingramcontent.com/pod-product-compliance
Lightning Source LLC
Chambersburg PA
CBHW021358300426
44114CB00012B/1276